SEA ROOM
by
R. A. PARSONS

SEA ROOM

BY

R. A. PARSONS

Published by
THE NEWFOUNDLAND ARTS CENTRE
DUCKWORTH STREET
ST. JOHN'S, NEWFOUNDLAND

Printed and bound in Canada
T. H. Best Printing Company Limited

Dedication

To

SIR JOHN CHALKER CROSBIE, K.B.E.

1876 - 1932

Who in his private capacity and as Minister of Shipping contributed so much to the industrial life of Newfoundland, particularly to the revival and extension of our shipping.

Foreword

Hon. Sir Brian Edward Spencer Dunfield, Kt.,
Judge of the Supreme Court of Newfoundland

I have long been accustomed to receive from my old friend Mr. Richard Augustus Parsons, Q.C., B.C.L., prosaic documents, entitled sometimes "Statement of Claim" and sometimes "Defence"; and on these documents I have long been accustomed to pronounce what might be called the Afterword. Now I receive from him documents of a very different kind, yet equally realistic; and on them he asks me to pronounce a Foreword; an introduction, not a judgment.

We in the Maritime Provinces, of which Newfoundland is now one, are very familiar with the sea: it dominates all our thinking. From childhood we have looked out to the East and South and watched ships, seamen, fishermen. We older ones, like the author and myself, have seen things through to the age of mechanization; and we see around us now only the remnants of the way of life of an earlier day. Yet the folk-ways do not alter so fast. The fishers and small-ship sailors of Newfoundland, as of our sister Eastern Provinces, formed and still form a world of their own far removed from that of the city dweller or country man of the mainland.

It is good therefore that an elder Newfoundlander, such as Mr. Parsons, should seek to crystalize in rhyme some vision of that way of life before it passes altogether. Our author knows it well, and conveys the atmosphere of that world, especially when his characters give utterance in the style of speech and thought so familiar to us all.

I commend Mr. Parsons' contribution, not his first, to the rather scanty literature of this Island Province.

Brian Dunfield.

St. John's, Nfld., June 8th, 1962.

Contents

The author wishes to thank Mr. Richard Greene, B.A., for the assistance given him in the preparation of this little volume.

ILLUSTRATIONS BY
PAUL PARSONS

SEA ROOM

"The Storm"

Hard weather, getting worse and worse,
South West the wind a gale,
Tough time for ships at sea tonight;
And schooners old or frail,
While daylight holds should run for it
And make a harbor soon,
Or keep away and snug 'em down
With lots of good sea room.

But ill's that wind that blows no good,
And this one as I judge,
Will stifle all fair weather snarls
And many a foc'sle grudge.
For when the common enemy,
With maw agape shall wait
The op'ning seams, the choking pumps,
Who trifles with his hate?

As for myself, I like a storm,
That is occasion'lly,
When I'm beleaguered by **restraint,**

And much propriety;
A storm the need whereof for days
The languid airs complain,
And moan and whine at last to burst
With sheets of driving rain;
That meets me on the open ground
And flails me as I stride,
Until I reach my cabin door
And slam the door inside!

A storm that makes the stove pipe blush
Bombards my lowly roof,
Yet cannot breach what I've made sure
Is wind and weather proof.

A storm that flushes holes and ponds
To banish filth and slime,
That cleanses ev'ry highway hedge
And routs the dust and grime!

I like a storm, it heartens me,
As with expedient rude
I circumvent its vagaries
And am with joy imbued.
I like a storm when we contrive
To make the very least
Go far enough, with gratitude,
To make a merry feast.

I like the wind, I lean upon,
Disputing ev'ry pace,
I like the rain on winds Southwest,
That drives against my face!

I like a storm; it routs the gloom
That suffocates the mind,
Reveals the naked verities,
To me and all mankind;
Expels the shams a little while,
And cuts men down to size,
As vanity submits to worth,
And foolish men to wise.

I like a storm, I know its grace,
And wholly I agree
With many a storm, were I assured
That ships were safe at sea!

My Little Town

Upon the headlands we may fairly view
The harbour and the town that by it grew,
Sustained by tiny farms and fisheries,
And not a little by home industries
Through centuries; and there be those yet hale
Amongst us yet who can recount the tale
Of fifty ships, that cleared the port and bore
In early June along the Labrador;
Of vessels too, that skunned their way to hunt
For seals in March out on the Gulf and Front;
But there was time aplenty ev'ry year
To fence and cultivate the lands 'bout here
And livyers tilled, to gather ample yields,
Their kitchen gardens and potato fields;
And ev'ry fam'ly then, if wiser now,
Was pleased to keep a hog or two and cow
And in the strength of young and ancient hands
Stacked high the hay upon its meadow lands.
Then sang the spinning wheel, and many a skill
The lamp-lit hours of winter months would fill.

19

How well the multi-coloured mats in frame
Became the hearth, that shone with logs aflame.
With home cured bacon, hams and butter pure
And garden viands, of such taste no more,
Withal wild berries, that about here grew,
The family then a wholesome larder knew.

But we must not permit the past to bind,
To choke or clutter or confuse the mind.
The town has grown and progressed, for 'tis said
It does not bother now with home-baked bread.

The kitchen garden, as 'twas fondly known,
The prime resource and sustenance of home,
Through generations tended, now is gone,
Or lies untilled, abandoned and forlorn,
As sons irrev'rent of a frugal age
Or scornful of their landed heritage,
Reject the guaranty for which it stood,
Through stress and failure, as a source of food;
And as more prosp'rous now, but far less sage,
Confide their future to inconstant wage.

But few now match the boards their fathers spread
Of crops they raised and meat their lush grass fed;
Though of their confidence I'm bound to say,
There's far more traffic now around our bay,

As vans and trucks a hurried schedule run
In tinned and bottled goods, from sun to sun.

That they have progressed and deserve great praise
For their advancement from their sires' ways,
We do confess; but yet regret to find
That in their haste, they've left rare wealth behind.

Capital Punishment

The man was tried, found guilty, and 'twas meet
That he should die. Conducted without heat.
The trial was fair, the Judge discreet,
Considerate. The jury in retreat
Spent twice the time required to arrive
Upon a verdict, but could not contrive
Substantial grounds for doubt. And in due course
The court oblivious of the aweful Source
Of this man's life, declared in accents dread
That he must hang, and by the neck, till dead;
Although, as seemed, of some misgivings droll,
Judically took notice of his soul.
'Twas but a mockery he felt to preach
About a thing that dwelt beyond its reach
And that it might not kill, for it was clear
It saw no way to let Him meddle here;
And pious motions could no wise deceive
This man it left the devil to reprieve,
Dividing life, irrev'rent of the whole
And of the Source and journey of the Soul.

The Three Brothers

(To the Honourable Eli Dawe, Captain John
Dawe and William Dawe Esquire, Manufacturer)

I knew and can recall the brothers three,
When they had well nigh finished with the sea.
Affection can grave faults repair in time,
And through long years known crudities refine;
But I, as one dispassionate of pen,
Mark down and limn, as I appraised them then
Who were, as I can well remember them,
Of middle height, broad shouldered, bearded men.

Their eyes were grey, of contemplative gaze
And humourous, though truculent in ways;
But yet their thicket brows, then sear in age,
Achieved for all appearance gen'ral sage.

By nature steadfast, it was sometimes thought
They held opinions longer than they ought;
But there were few who held they would contend,
For what they might not honestly defend.

'Twas ever felt and none thought to dispute
That they deserved amongst us, high repute:
Their word was as their bond. None dared suspect
That once 'twas given, it would not be kept;
Nor did they misuse English to invent
Or twist the meaning of their covenant;
And they were punctual, and held that wine
Posed no excuse for stealing others time.
Their speech had purpose, not for waste on prate,
Or to dissemble or prevaricate.

Folks copied them, and sought their sound advice,
Which in disputes, all factions would suffice —
In short, the three, as we looked to them then,
Were all Godfearing, honest gentlemen —

It is not strange, that we in exercise
Of rights and privileges, should recognize,
And by our suffrages, make known our choice
Of one, who would in council give us voice;
And thus the eldest of the people's will,
Served in their House with honour and with skill;
And proved in council wise and competent,
Went on to office high in government.

As for the second, till enfeebled, he
Held to the last by his first love the sea,

And sailed his "Dauntless" on, till she no more
Could meet the gales and tides of Labrador.

The last of these, who early quit the sea
Turned with zeal to trade and industry,
And by his wit and wise experiment
Improved the standing of our settlement,
And by the commerce that he gave the town
Brought it prosperity, himself renown.
He was a shrewd and calculating man
Forever disinclined to skip and scan;
Yet never faltered, when he once began,
But wrought persistently, by his known plan.

Some doubtless will define all men as great,
Who render special service to the State
To gain the praise of President or Queen
Presidium or Heads of some regime,
Disposed to right and justice — or to hate —
Who value service as their ends dictate;
While others so appraise all, that deserve
The thanks of thousands, they unselfish serve.

Perchance, they all are great; but for my part,
The matter lies much nearer to the heart —
We do not ask the nation to debate
Or leave the question to a potentate;

Our next door neighbour, we suppose, is great
If him in virtue, we may imitate.

When good men passed, your fathers of respect
Tall monuments were minded to erect,
To bring great deeds or virtues back to mind,
That you therein a way of life might find;
But though the three, whose honour I maintain
No plaque nor column have to praise their fame,
They, notwithstanding, how we demonstrate
Or test the quality of being great,
Laid hold of virtues, we may imitate
Or wrought in manner, we may emulate.

Early Ploughing

Early Ploughing

This Spring they're early at their ploughing here
On Warford's land, though 'tis a backward year,
And frost's still in the earth and I'll be bound,
There's just as much in his, as our ground;
But he was ever yarry, and somehow
His boys are eager set, as he, to plough
And rouse the soil, to find no better worth,
Than pleasant odours of the fresh turned earth.
And there's no sense at all to seed the land
Till come full moon; but on the other hand,
Although they do, as others here, complain
Of early heart-break labour to no gain,
There must be something, that they find in this,
These Warford men, that we must somehow miss.

Lines to the Robin

Through March and most of April ev'ry year
The winds blow on our land around 'bout here
From North, Northeast and from the East, or veer
From point to point along that quadrant drear;
And though 'tis drawing close to May month now
The ground is hardly ready for the plough
And if the trees of habit change their dress
And shoot their buds, they still look comfortless;
But Robin's here. He came in overnight!
We saw him working by first sunlight
And calling with such urgency of voice;
We knew his love had left him little choice.

'Tis just a legend, but it holds that thou
Didst draw a thorn from our Lord Jesu's brow,
And of the stream that welled incarnadine
Didst find a glory for that breast of thine.

We have no means whereby we may attest
The Olden Order of the Scarlet Vest
But as the lives of ancients we construe

From all we know of them, what more they do,
Compounding legends, so perchance it grew
Of kindness that the ancients found in you;
And though the lark in song may heavenward fare,
And singing, soar beyond all human care,
The better part is thine, O Robin dear,
For thou hast winged the grace of heaven here.

The Gloucesterman

I watched him as he patched his ancient mill
In early Spring, at ev'ning, and until
He stood at ease, as he discovered me
And came my way in smiling courtesy;
And at that moment, 'twould have been a joy
To paint, had I been able to employ
The tricks of brush that painters use to stress
Those features that the character confess,
Or skills they practice to arrest and bind
Some glory transient, that they instant find.
The man was tall, a trifle bent, and lean,
In woodsman's denim clad and faded jean.
His eyes were clear as mountain pools, deep set
In shadow of his thicket brows of jet.
His hair was plentiful, unused to care
Save of the winds, that brushed it anywhere.
Though sluiced by rain and sleet, and seamed and lined
By ev'ry torture of the Northern wind,
His rugged countenance was not unkind,
And bore assurance of a tranquil mind.

For this was Matthew Rorke, whom haply you
Recall, as I, or whom your fathers knew
When he was younger, and who can
Inform you surely of the Gloucesterman,
For in his early years, he trawled off shore
And fished the Banks from schooners here, and more
He sailed on pogey voyages far away
Along Pacific Coasts and made good pay;
Though he came back and knocked about in trade
And off and on Atlantic voyages made;
But quit, and took to "going up around"
Where pay was higher; vessels better found
And years and years till, middle age, he made
As much as any fisherman was paid
Aboard a Gloucesterman, for proven worth
Assured him ev'ry season of a berth
Upon a ship as staunch and as well found
As any vessel from New England bound.

He had been long content, where he could earn
An ample wage and render in return
A labour equal, constant in the will
To serve with diligence and ready skill.
But spent of grief, suspicion or a grudge,
The finest artisan becomes a drudge,
And thus despite his reputation there,
He came to find his old employment drear

36

At last, and altogether without joy,
As restive grown, of grieving for his boy.

A son, who in his early years revealed
A spirit bold, and in the playing field,
By reason of his strength, endurance, skill,
Gained admiration and withal good will,
For he was kind by nature and was fair,
Despite pre-eminence amongst boys here,
Who in his splendid years of youth gave o'er
To none in prowess at the sweep and oar
Who sensed their functions and employed all sails,
To use and humour the inconstant gales;
And carried on, a confidant of storm,
Or as a child unto the tempest born.

Though Matthew Rorke himself preferred the sea,
With its employments, to the land; yet he
Was not inclined, or so it would appear
From words he dropped in conversation here
Amongst his friends, to let his son and heir
Embrace the hardships that our seamen bear,
And thus he shipped in foreign ports each year
And made good money with a bit to spare
To school his son, who would in time secure
Some sal'ried post desirable ashore;
But skiffs and schooners from the far off days
Since first they seawards slid on ancient ways,

Have held a charm, more subtle than the sway
Of steady wage on boys "reared 'round the bay".

And Martin took to dories in the way
Of other youngsters here, as for his play,
And got to rowing, awkwardly at first,
But dextrously in time, as he rehearsed
The part of grown men in that exercise,
And copied those he chose to recognize
For skill therein, or fancied more than most;
Though all were skilled along Trepassey coast.
And more, he learned to discipline his craft
In stormy seas; equipped with sail and mast.
And as to vig'rous sturdy youth he grew,
He gained a skill in sailing here, that few
His age might emulate; and without kin
To share the voyage as dory mate with him,
He, though unbid of need or urgent call,
Save that of venture, would 'till late in fall,
Sail on the grounds to tend and pay out trawl,
Or go wherever fish might run or haul.
And ever venturing, he went afar,
The mounting seas, or fogs banked high to bar
Unhindering, as though at all times bent,
To find excitement and whereof content.
His life seemed charmed. His trips gave none concern,
Until he made the voyage of no return.

And Matthew Rorke, his father, tired grown
Of grief in loneliness, desired home.
So to his master, he recounted o'er
The tale, his "old man" likely heard before
From other mouths, and something of the grief,
That harried him and pressed for that relief,
He sought. With commendations, he deserved,
He quit the vessel, he so long had served,
Stowed all his odds and ends and bits of gear,
Farewelled his seamates and commenced to fare
To Newfoundland, to work amongst his own
And wait, convinced that Martin would come home.
To think his boy had gone for evermore
Or perished, he most steadfastly forebore.
His valiant spirit constantly would strive
To keep his son within his heart alive,
For he of need must have his boy survive
All ills that men or demons might connive;
On no account would he acceptance give
To black despair, for his beloved must live.

Indiff'rent crews abandonment dictate;
The faithful, though she sink, yet hesitate.
'Twere like a stranger only, to invent
Or good or evil, as indifferent.
'Twixt life and death, 'twixt good and evil fate,
A father surely may not arbitrate.
He chose survival, yet in faith he prayed

The hand of evil might all times be stayed,
And till a father's prayers should prove in vain,
He would expect to see his son again.
At all events, he would at length be home;
The only port, from whence, 'twas surely known,
His boy had made departure, and from there
His eyes would search the seas about, and bear
Upon the passing ships, and with these veer,
Till each, of course assigned, should disappear
Beneath his horizons; for in his view,
To watch and pray was all that he might do,
Beyond his toil for those necessities,
Whereof resource lay in his neighb'ring seas.

When we have witnessed death, or we have been
Convinced of this, that others must have seen,
We passively acknowledge then an end,
Beyond our wit or wisdom to amend;
And mourn a while, for death must know a night
Of grief; but there is sorrow infinite
For him, we've loved, last heard employed afar
On peaceful missions or engaged in war
Reported missing, or for him we've bred,
That strangers now would have us deem as dead,
Whom we may not, though reason we defy,
Till that reluctant spark within us die,
And pray we must, though from the dusk till dawn,
Our counsel varied bid us hope or mourn

For him we've lost, denied alone of voice
To reach us through the agony of choice;
And were he done with night or ev'ning here,
Must we regard him now proscribed of prayer
Or of our intercessions? Who in grief
Bereavéd thus, although of unbelief
Confessed, or blatant of an untried creed,
Is scornful, conscious of the present need,
His nature innate hath to intercede;
Or doth not overt, or in secret plead?

And they who pray do not unlikely find
A consolation or some peace of mind.
These view a mighty Father as their Source
Though skeptics pose a cold unyielding Force.
They know or feel they can be understood
And sense a God compassionate and good,
Who them hath fashioned made; for verily,
Not they themselves, who ever He may be,
And hold 'tis not in reason, sons create
Who laugh, shed tears, who love and even hate,
Should uncontending calmly contemplate
Their own Creator cold dispassionate;
And hold indeed though reason order plead
And ev'ry consequence a cause concede,
That none doth err, who of his case extreme
Pray that the all wise God may intervene,
And though he urge his cause again, again,

And all his importunities seem vain,
Communion with his God may prove a meed
Above all benisons he conscious plead.

How strange it turns for on that very day
He quit his ship, a thousand miles away
A little girl had strayed, and none knew where;
But none thought far, because her feet were bare
And she was lightly clad; and likely few
Would dream the journey of a child of two,
Might lie beyond the village, or without
The lanes and pleasant gardens thereabout
Her home at Colinet. She walked at dawn
Along the lanes by meadow, garden, lawn,
Before Hugh's mill had blown its early blast,
Or stirred a soul to break his nightly fast.
She went her ways as by enchantment borne,
Before the mists had from the pastures gone,
And cattle there contrived to let her pass
Or broused, absorbed, the dew revivéd grass;
But whither? No one could profess
That his was better than another's guess.

'Twas nigh on noon, ere neighbours were disposed
To take alarm, and then the village rose,
As one. The mill, the store and school were closed
And all agreed, for it was so proposed
For those assembled, swiftly to extend

And ev'ry hillock climb and vale descend
And search with diligence each nook and nest
That offered shelter or invited rest;
And with that eagerness, remarked in hounds,
They coursed and thrashed the valleys and the mounds.
The marshes, swamps, and dry and barren grounds.
And miles and miles beyond the village bounds,
They traipsed along the rivers, lakes and ponds
And searched beneath their weeds and reeds and fronds.
Day after day, by weather unconfined,
They sought the maid, till they became resigned
To failure or exhaustion claimed their mind,
Or reason, in the circumstance, declined
All further search, for then to all 'twas clear
That she had perished in the waters here,
Or passed from life within the forests near,
Or yet had drifted on the morning air
Into the void or infinite and left
Conjecture only, to her friends bereft.

And there were those who said, and yet who say,
Of their belief, unto this very day,
That fairies led the little girl astray
And nourished her in their mysterious way;
For we have old and wise men, who agree,
That there be little men, we cannot see,
Who yet inhabit forest lands and hide
Amid the valleys of the countryside,

43

And ancients now, who solitary make
Long journeys through the woodlands, take
Some little offerings in meat or cake,
The gnomes and fairies to propitiate
And leave these here and there by boughs of green
Observed by none, save little men unseen.

We do not wish, my masters, nor do you
His trip from Gloucester homeward to pursue,
But that our tale be better understood,
We join Matt Rorke again at Holyrood,
From whence, if he's bound home, his course must bear
Along the road that forks at Salmonier,
One branch to run along St. Joseph's way,
Preferred by those bound to Trepassey Bay;
The other bent to Colinet, and found
To favour travellers, Placentia bound.

Rorke rode the twenty miles to Salmonier
And strange, though it may seem, dismounted there,
Paid what was then the customary fare
Received and housed his trav'ling box and gear.
Took kettle, food (enough to serve the road),
And with this light equipage, forthwith strode
Not to the left, but in the roadway right
To Colinet, to lodge there overnight;
For of sound reason, or a forceful mood,
Constrained or felt on reaching Holyrood,

He had determined with despatch to mend
A long neglect and to reclaim a friend,
For whom he bore affection then as one
Who was his father's only other son,
And would though no man else might see its sense
Confirm and buttress Matthew's confidence.
And of this mind, he set off to atone
His absence long, and find his brother's home
At Colinet, that lay ten miles away
And where, he did not doubt, the night he'd stay
And find occasion there to spend next day,
And morning, if he did not tarry there,
Rejoin the road he quit at Salmonier,
Resume his journey by St. Joseph's way.
Thence by St. Mary's to Trepassey Bay.

His good intentions made his journey light.
The sun shone from a sky, nigh cloudless bright
About his path, that wandered in the shade
Of bord'ring trees, then on by marshes, made
Desirable of all their wild perfumes,
Prepared from roots and grasses, plants and blooms
Innumerable, and borne today from these,
With constancy upon the gentle breeze.
The birds gave out occasion'lly in song
And eased his trav'ling on the roadway long.
But open air and exercise 'tis trite
Can tantalize the weakest appetite.

45

So as he'd trudged so far, he felt inclined
To eat, where other travellers had dined
Not long ago, beside a fine clear stream
And by a rock o'erhanging that must seem
Upreared for shade and by the earth out thrown
Prepared and sculptured for that purpose lone.
Hard by the other border of the stream
There was a wood, to which there might be seen
An opening or entrance to a way,
That ran how far within, he could not say,
Because the wood was thick and bound to hide
The pathway through it, howsoever wide.
The place looked good, and so he moved with haste
To shift his gear, reform the fireplace,
To gather wood and lay it, so to draw
Or take advantage of the gentlest flaw.
How sweet the scent of wood smoke to the soul
Of men grown tired, wishful to be whole,
And oh, betwixt us both, just you and me,
How good is salt cured cod, with bread and tea!

'Tis strange, that those who have so hardly wrought,
Tough handed men, by gentle arts untaught,
Renouncing such, as wasteful of their time,
Do, notwithstanding their professed design,
Compulsive, turn to yarn and song and rhyme,
As you, more learned or leisured may incline

"As, one by one, they ventured forth to view"

To opus, saga, or to verse sublime,
Urged of that thirst within us all, divine.

And there's a kinship that we find within,
When we are lonely, as we try to win
The confidence, as from a little child,
The trust of some small creature of the wild;
And thus, he closely watched the jay that flew
From tree to tree, the while, it nearer drew,
As confidence and trust within it grew,
Towards the crumbs the lonely stranger threw.
Observed as well its lurking retinue,
As, one by one, they ventured forth to view
The man beneficent, disposed to fare
On what he surely wished with them to share,
Of his discernment of the hunger they
In common felt with him of creature clay.

What thoughts assail us when we walk alone,
If we are ever thus, for ev'ry stone
And ev'ry stick provoke long questions then
About themselves and of the scope of men;
On such occasions is our time well spent,
For ev'ry woodnote then is reverent.
In His vast peace all things both great and small,
Unto the least of these that creep and crawl,
Perform their office though they only wait
Until their several cycles must abate.

Paul Parsons '62

"He saw a tiny girl"

All things of earth, the furthest star, the sun,
And space itself, although diverse, are one.
'Tis wisdom then to worship and to own
Our triune God, who plans in love alone.

When he had eaten and had drunk his fill,
He filled and lit his pipe and smoked until
A drowsiness, like that of one long tossed
By seas, or careless grown of worlds well lost,
Crept close beside, within him, and he slept
Until it seemed, he dreamed of one who wept,
Then wakened drowsily to hear a cry,
That might have come from far, or low, heard nigh,
He could not say. He waited quietly
To find out most assuredly, if he
Had heard aright. He heard again the cry,
A little cry, as of a child, from nigh
And looking to the entrance to the wood,
He saw a tiny girl. Nor cloak nor hood
Wore she, and viewed from slight advantage here,
She gave the notion, that her feet were bare.

How strange indeed her presence to him seemed!
Was he awake, or sleeping still, and dreamed?
And of his dreams, too vivid, did invent
This child, so far from any settlement?
For though he had been trav'ling long, he yet
Was four miles off or more from Colinet;

But though awake or dreaming, never had
He seen a wraith so robed, or child thus clad
In such a setting, or so far from home,
Without companions, utterly alone.
Awake indeed, convinced he did not dream,
He called the maid, and slowly crossed the stream.

In little time he reached her by the wood,
Then kneeled beside her, to be understood
He came as friend, and in his way beguiled
Her fears suspect. The little maiden smiled
On his rough arts. As he removed alarm
And lulled her fears, he sought about for harm
Or wounds, and finding none, he bathed her face
And gath'ring up the little maid in haste,
He bore her, restful, to his fire-place
And from his food prepared, with tenderness
And skill unthought, a tasty little mess.

When she had eaten, he, though without care
At all for his, brushed awkwardly her hair,
As a propriety, though unaware
That it was beautiful, abundant, fair.
When he had done with this, he noted she
Who'd borne his ministrations patiently,
Would sleep, and growing cautious of the sun,
He raised in haste the slumb'ring little one

Upon his arm, and burdened thus, he set,
With some concern, his course for Colinet.

Few were the travellers he saw that day,
And not a soul as he resumed his way
To Colinet; but as the road began
To thread the settlement, he saw a man,
Who joined the roadway from a garden nigh,
And paused, of course, to greet the passer-by,
As livyers do, though scornful men decry
The practice where our quiet roadways lie.
But these I ween should be together drawn
By instinct or by her the twain were borne;
Yet as they meet, the livyer stoops to stare,
With wid'ning eyes, upon the maiden fair,
For she, the trav'ler carries is no less
Than one thought dead, whose name you too may guess!

How strange is this, so strange that it must seem
He'd known her plight and voyaged to intervene;
But much proceeds from what we've schemed and
    planned
Beyond our wit to plumb or understand.
And you, my masters, if beyond belief
My tale may seem, inquiry make of Lucy Keefe
In Colinet of those, who knew her there
And yet recall the Gloucesterman and where,

He haply found the maiden trav'ling near
The road, due West, he chose at Salmonier.

Rorke told the livyer all, as unto one
Who was a stranger, not his father's son,
Of how he'd found the child an hour agone,
Adrift, as though abandoned, and had borne
The maiden hence; then heard as in exchange
The tale of Lucy's disappearance strange,
Of how she'd strayed, whilst neighbours were abed,
How she was sought, at last, presumed as dead.

Not till their tales were told, had either eyes
His own blood brother fond, to recognize
Then as sweet recognition on them grew,
And as surprise upon surprise each knew,
They like to boistrous youths late reconciled,
Gave forth, in voice so loud and gesture wild,
Their antics shook and woke the slumb'ring child,
Who notwithstanding on the brothers smiled.
Abruptly roused to reason by her smile,
And well aware, within a scanty mile
A family mourned, and of the house from whence,
The maiden strayed, with joy, they hurried thence.

Rorke told his tale again, and o'er and o'er,
One hundred times and like a hundred more,
He could not tell, he did not keep the score,

"Their antics shook and woke the slumbering child"

To those, who came to him from ev'ry door.
And came again to gather details more,
Or hear again what they had heard before
A dozen times, perchance already bent
To get the best in future argument.
When all his visitors had made for home
And he at last was in his room alone,
He pondered on the wonders of the day:
Upon the maiden he had found astray
And carried home; upon the entrance, he
A stranger, thither borne by tragedy
Along a thousand miles by land and sea,
Had made onto the stage unwittingly,
An entrance, timed precisely for the part
Assigned, played out too well for conscious art.
In some strange way he took it all, of sign
That Martin would return to him in time;
And he would wait, contented hence to keep
In resolution firm, then found he sleep.

He did not long in Colinet remain,
For he was anxious to again regain
The road to Salmonier and make his way
To house and home within Trepassey Bay.
And in due course he reached his cottage there,
Repaired his stage and boat and fishing gear,
As he had meant to do, and made it clear
That he would carry on, as others here.

"Repaired his stage and boat and fishing gear"

At home, he did not idle in concern,
Or bide inactive, till his son's return;
But set to work, until his fishing gear
Resembled that of other livyers there,
No less than Bridget's household wares inclined
To bring full fifty kitchens there to mind;
All spacious, and with furniture and gear,
Designed for lux'ry less than honest wear,
Yet fostered so, or furbished in such sheen,
As from these rooms all drabness to redeem.

Of its belongings, let us pause to view:
The great old barrel-ovened Waterloo,
Designed to comfort, bake, to boil and stew,
To all of these employments varied, true;
With grace, beyond its offices assigned,
To proffer solace and compose the mind
And of the flare and flicker of its beams
To raise and fashion palaces of dreams;
The long "low settle", in ship's canvas bound;
With soft warm covers and gay cushions found;
And save its edging, narrow and kept bare,
The plancheon spread with homemade rugs, now rare,
To be removed instanter, at the chance
Of fun or frolic in some old square dance;
The baise spread table, rocker, gen'ral chairs;
The dresser tall, with ancient lusterwares;

And with all these, to gentle and to charm,
A simple kindliness, forthright and warm.

As they who treasure find in works obscure
Or rediscover splendours that endure,
We find that Bridget Rorke, as we review
Her conduct now, had worth we never knew,
For though she was inclined to wear her hair
Too tightly drawn, reluctant to appear
As frivolous; to let her brown eyes rare
Renounce their smiles for frowns less comely there;
And seemed severe with those disposed to bear
Of indolence, misfortune in despair,
She was most gentle with the worthy, kind
Unto the valiant, for we call to mind,
That she would tend upon and nurse the ill
And of her ready wit and natural skill,
The offices of surgeon would fulfil
And treat the wounds and fractured limbs, until
These healed, or till the doctor came 'long here
On one of his uncertain calls each year;
And furthermore of herbs and roots that grew
Around about the place, would steep and brew
The remedies she gave for this and that disease,
For aches and pains, without a thought of fees;
And though she might occasion'lly, intent
In preparation of medicament,
Unstable grown of some ingredient,

Disposed in course of nature to fermenī,
Allow her brew, in cause of science bent,
To stray beyond the statut'ry content,
No constable or J. P. worth the name
Would be disposed her practice to restrain;
And berries would she pick, toward the fall,
To jam and jar and shelve and share with all,
Who through no fault of theirs might stand in need.
Or had an illness or complaint to plead;
And little children too, were sometimes fed
At Bridget's board with jam and homemade bread;
O Bridget was a woman in her time,
Like your own mother, I suppose, and mine!

And Michael Rorke went to the fishing ground
And late and early wrought, as one who's bound
To take no part at all, save to excel
In labours chosen, or perform these well.
But though surcease from sorrow thus be found,
Something or other, sensed of sight or sound,
Might on occasions, urgent as the whirr
Of wings pursued in panic, rouse and stir
His consciousness, arresting ev'ry thought,
Save that of his loved son, for whom he sought;
And then the image of his son would rise,
Of countenance familiar, and of guise,
Well known, apparelled as he ought
In circumstance, although of fancy wrought;

Of gaze, he loved too well, to recognize
Without a poignancy to rheum his eyes,
Renouncing verity; but 'twould recur
No whit, in form or lineament, to err,
On like occasion or unthought event,
Through labour, leisure, wheresoe'er he went.

They rarely spoke of Martin in the home,
Though he and Bridget spent long whiles alone
Each spouse, most likely, careful to refrain
From what was bound to give the other pain;
Or they were minded to perhaps conceal
The doubts they might in converse there reveal,
Or yet would simulate their unconcern
In silence, certain of their son's return;
And visitors aware how both inclined,
Would not, intending, bring their boy to mind,
And through their conversation would forebear
To speak at all of Martin's absence there.
And Bridget worked as Matthew, and as he,
Found refuge in her proper industry;
Yet as disposed, or as accustomed, she
Would pause at times to ponder on the sea.

What secrets hath the sea! What doth it hide
Of its immensity, commotion, tide?
What hath it garnered, covert, to withhold,
Since first the gathered waters lapped and rolled

"Would pause at times to ponder on the sea"

Along primeval coasts in Earth's dim past,
To be released at leisure, or at last;
What hath it hid within recorded time,
To be dissolved and lost to all design,
Or kept beyond remembrance and released,
When all enquiry or concern here ceased?
And those few tokens, that the seas concede,
We have no wit at all, or wish, to read,
For we have heard about the ship, or knew
The vessel missing, posted overdue,
Would, in her fragments here of driftwood, see
No more than largess in anonymity.
And with this child, late orphaned by the storm,
Would undiscerning, by its fires warm.

From Cape Race to St. Mary's, there's a shore,
Whereof our old men speak, and still, with awe,
Although familiar grown with death and storm;
With helpless vessels, falsely reck'ning, borne,
Confused in fog and far off course astray,
On tides that sweep toward Trepassey Bay;
With sundered spars and tangled trailing gear;
With gallantry, with death, too near for fear,
And with the wreck of these, that rusts and rots
Along the rocks and reefs that spur St. Shott's.

Three days ago, "the Hector" staunch and hale,
Three hundred tons in burthen and in sail,

Rigged schoonerwise, though used to ocean trade,
Ten hands all told, with gen'ral cargo lade,
Cleared Halifax, then bound for Carbonear,
To load in salt cod, on discharging there.
Her crew were Newfoundlanders all, save one
And he signed on at Malaga, but none
At all could this man's place of birth decide,
Or where his kin or people might reside;
But as adrift, and as the flotsam flung
Upon the beach, and of an Irish tongue,
Or lilting brogue, he had the way to please
The master, then shorthanded, by decease
Of one A. B. and so inclined to heed,
A likely lad abandoned and in need
Of consul; (but what nation's no one knew)
And thus he shipped to join " the Hector's" crew
And with a knack for handling sail and gear,
The wheel, in wind or wave, and skill to steer
Along the calm for ev'ry capful there,
Withal good humour and the sense to bear
The chipping, painting, scrubbing, mending here,
He served her, voyage on voyage, nigh on three year.

The day he joined the ship, three years ago,
He bore a scar, then hardly healed to show
A desp'rate injury along his scalp and brow,
Sustained at sea; but said, he knew not how.

63

He could recall so little, for in truth
He had no boyhood or remembered youth.

His life commenced in consciousness restored
Somehow, amongst a motley crew aboard
A powered schooner running rum and beer
Somewhere, he later reasoned, off St. Pierre.

He must have spent a fortnight, likely more,
Upon a bunk afforred, insecure,
Uncertain of his company, although
They did no doubt some rough concern bestow;
For, time to time the cook would come below,
Occasion'lly, the skipper, to bestow
Attentions in the way of off'ring food
Or treatment, "s'posed to do a power of good,"
Until he left his bunk and learned to stand;
But then, with his recovery at hand,
A fire broke out abaft, at night, that blew
Her deck apart and swept her half-dazed crew
In panic 'board the tender, which she drew,
And in abandonment, for all they knew
Or likely cared, of him, to certain doom,
Within the confines of his forred room;
For they were hidden by the clouded night,
Beyond the borders of the fire light,

Ere he had climbed upon the twisted deck
To seek some means to quit the blazing wreck.

And means, he said, he then most strangely found,
For from the quarter, there but lightly bound,
The dory had been lifted clear and hurled
To windward 'forred, where her painter curled
About the ship's cathead, and held her tight
As though arrested in her wayward flight!

He told how he had stumbled in this boat,
Viewed safe as any skiff her size afloat
As seamen hold the dory ev'rywhere;
But his had very little running gear,
Beyond her iron rations, held secure
Within a metal cuddy small; one oar,
A trifle splintered, as the boat was flung;
Another one, its fellow, seized, as sprung
From over or misuse, but helpful still
And for some time, if used with mod'rate skill;
An old tarpaulin, torn from its late use,
As shade for her, against the sun's abuse.
No mast or gaff to rig a sail had he,
Or other means to ease his way at sea;
But he was fortunate, he thought, to find
The means he had, to leave the hell behind;
And he, with these and nothing more beside,
Preferred the way of wind and weather tide

To that of those, heard fitfully in flight,
Beyond the circle of the flaming night,
And felt that, somehow of his drifting, he
Would come upon the trade routes of the sea.

Rain fell next day and this, he said, he caught
Upon the old tarpaulin, and with thought
He carefully conserved it, to avail
Against the tardiness of smoke or sail
In rising from his horizons, for he,
With knowledge scant of his locality,
And less of merchant routes about the sea,
Could only wait upon delivery.

For nigh a week, the mock of wind and tide,
And none, with him, the watches to divide,
In fear of sleep, for slumber well might hide
The vessels sought, and dreams had lately lied,
He waited. Then, as one to be denied
Of rescue, he but waited to abide
The end, resigned, too tired to divide
The false and true; yet waiting thus, descried
A ship, which he was minded to deride
As phantasy, until a seaman cried!
Yes 'twas a ship. He still could see the sail!
He heard again! It was the seaman's hail!

And just as often as he told his tale,
Of that long drift and drear, in search of sail,
He heard that cry indeed, for none might fail
To note, as he rehearsed that seaman's hail,
That he would gaze, as on the narrowing seas
Betwixt his dory and the "Skudanese,"
A square rigged ship, Norwegian or a Dane,
In cargo laden, destined then for Spain.

He never found it easy to explain
His wanderings in Malaga; but vain,
Oh vain he knew, were effort to regain
That land he'd lost, whereof he knew no name;
To find some consulate, whereon to claim
Viaticum or other right maintain.

But lacking wit or wish to forge or feign,
Forlorn, frustrate of foreign tongues, he came,
As by some instinct moved and borne, to stand
Before a ship that hailed from Newfoundland:
A vessel staunch and sensate of the share
In voyage and peril she should surely bear;
An honest ship, with friendly foc'sle smell
That on the exile spent its gracious spell;
A crew content (should ships possess the way,
That houses have, their tenants to portray).

"And long sought memories—returned to him"

And now this ship, he'd joined three years agone,
Full four days out of Halifax, in storm
Had sprung her mainmast; and by tempest torn,
A block, from tackle swinging loose, was borne
Upon young Kelly, and in such a way,
It left a wound, nigh where his old scar lay:
But strange to say, almost beyond belief,
His last misfortune gave his first relief,
For as a surgeon, cruel to be kind,
His latest injury restored his mind,
And long sought memories, he wished in proof
Of birth, of boy and manhood, of the roof
That was his father's, of his kith and kin
That he supposed had long abandoned him,
And of his voyage by dory on that day
So long ago, as confident and gay
He sailed in sun and tarried far away
As fog crept in and blanketed the Bay
Of that forgetfulness of all his past,
As suddenly there loomed and lounged the craft
Upon his boat and with a dev'lish art,
Destroyed the skiff and split his life apart,
RETURNED TO HIM, as to one roused from sleep,
Or as revived, late rescued, from the deep.

With no abatement of the storm, or sign,
His battered ship, then standing off Cape Pine,

"As suddenly there loomed and lounged the craft"

The master wary of her present plight
And of the weather worsening that night
Prepared to take his vessel in the Bay,
And harbor in Trespassey until day.

And as the vessel stretched and tacked and wore
Towards then, off, along the rugged shore,
The seaman, known as Kelly, heretofore
Unmindful of the injury he bore,
Was seen to look upon, as one who scanned
The sea about him, and the flinty strand,
With more delight than his who must decide
Upon the force and conduct of the tide;
Or more than his, who's bidden to survey
And chart the waters of Trepassey Bay;
And as the Hector to the harbour drew
And cottages and stages came in view,
His eyes with fever or emotion shone
Or lustrous grew of lamps he looked upon
In houses there, or of one lamp alone
That seaward burned to meet him sailing home.

Enough my masters, for you now must see
The close of Martin's jumbled odyssey;
No need of more, for with the harbour won
The Gloucesterman may hold again his son!
And Matthew Rorke, his son to him restored
Knows joy as one to whom it's been assured,

"That seaward burned to meet him sailing home"

Or as one seized of confidence sublime,
Who finds the faith he's held confirmed by time:
Thus as he looks upon his son again,
In flesh or phantom, he is calm and sane,
And grasps his hand and speaks but to caress
The name he loves, then kneels in thankfulness.

To Charlie (A Tabby Cat)

O Charlie boy, I do not think, you knew,
Or we ourselves, how much we cared for you;
And now that you have left us and the strife
Of frantic traffic, that begrudged you life,
We are not sure, how much respect to pay,
Or of the rev'rence, that becomes your clay,
As we prepare this warm spring earth to lay
Your little body decently away;
And though in this, too mindful of the part
You had in offices so near our heart,
We may the fine proprieties offend,
We are content; for you O little friend
Deserve our fond remembrance for the way
You had from time to time, to make us gay:
By speech you used, your wishes to convey,
Or moods; for who, as you, could so portray,
Composure, dignity; or, as you, burn,
With indignation, anger or concern;
And who as you, in this or any time,
Could clown as well or deal in pantomime?

For we have watched you sitting, in the roll
Of thinker and philosopher; then droll,
As you have sprung and capered in the mode
Of buffoon consummate, or as you strode,
With glowing eyes and fierce, your ears laid flat
In manner mindful of the autocrat;
Then just as easily, despite all that,
Resume the capers of the acrobat.

Oh you gave laughter, light; and if a thief,
You were by nature so, not of belief;
And oh my little friend, your life though brief,
Was not too narrow to encompass grief.

A Day on the Barrens

Dawn bursts upon the headlands seawardly,
Deprived of offices the moon goes in,
And morning spreads the barrens wide with light,
As vanishes the mist disposed to hide
The ponds and streams upon the Southern side
And stands of spruce along the valley North.

The wind is light, so light we scarcely trace
Its course, or sense its conflict with the face,
And pause awhile, as distantly we view
The western hills that climb to crests of blue.
So still and silent is it hereabout,
That I am almost now constrained to shout.
O God, how wondrous are Thy works and fair,
The gentle dawn and morning here declare.

But now my dog proceeds most cautiously
And I dare not frustrate his industry.
And of this dog?
Who lives and loves and is a part of this,
Of all its wonder and who shares my bliss,

Who ponders not nor tries to penetrate,
His origins or guess his future state,
Who doth not fear the chast'ning of Thy Rod,
But looks to me alone his creature god
For approbation or reproof.

And you my friend who would your dog abuse,
For some offence or lapse you can't excuse,
Trust not your wrath his manners to amend,
Or you, I think, more heinously offend;
But in your own behaviour calmly show,
(If thrash you must) the justice of your blow,
And if your discipline be fair and wise,
No grudge shall smolder or inflame his eyes;
From their great depths resentment shall not spring.
Or change the glance that first approved you king.

Dogs have their faults, no doubt; but one alone,
Has next to none when he becomes your own.
My dog is jealous and he can't abide,
His next of kin, who would my love divide;
He's given his I know, beyond recall,
And cannot share, for he has given all.

By pebbled ways through leaves now brown and red,
By shelving rock and alder clumps we tread;
We criss and cross the barrens, yet addressed
To places where we think the ground is best.

We understand each other, he and I
And hearts and minds are one as we draw nigh
And wait upon whatever yon may lie
To rise and fly, escape the blast, or die!
The scent is sharp; but sharp in sympathy
He shoots a covert rapid glance at me,
To note my stance. I whisper to assure
That I await, against surprise secure.

He hunts on ground, that I would hardly choose
And takes to ways and courses, I refuse.
Oh, we have diff'rences; but we divide
On issues fair, not just to take a side
As venal petty politicians do,
For we a common enterprise persue.

He knows, as well as I, a merry stream,
So well concealed 'tis heard before 'tis seen,
That wanders from an undetermined source,
And fills a little fountain in its course,
Within the shadow of a weathered stone,
Removed from kin, as there by tempest thrown,
And worn by ancient seas or by the hone
Of countless rains and winds that since have blown.

He knows as well the stone, that at its base
We'll find the ashes of our fire place;

And knows perchance within one hour's time,
That we, as long accustomed, there will dine,
But on the way we've "likely ground" to trace,
That may provide us with another brace!
I drop my pack and he reclines to trace,
My ev'ry movement at the fire place
Soon from the fagots I have gathered near,
And spread on boughs now tinder-dry appear,
As by magician conjured, flames that flare,
And throw their woodland incense on the air,
Then settle as the fagots in due course,
Glow steadfastly upon our hearth of gorse.

'Tis strange how simple things that we bring here,
This piping kettle purchased anywhere
For next to nothing, bits of cooking gear,
Of their environment, become so dear!
How this lone wilderness can so refine
The simple provender on which we dine!
As for myself, I would Olympus dare
To furnish forth ambrosia so rare,
For who would fail to favor such a dish,
As roasted sun-cured Petty Harbour fish!

The feast concludes; but some old hands advise,
Just now the birds are not inclined to rise,
We trust their wisdom, like it, and take we,
One golden hour of tranquility.

Respectful yet to his ancestral lore,
He does what he must do, has done before
A thousand times for reasons now obscure;
But we suppose, to make his couch secure,
So uses all four paws with great zest,
And flings the brush and gravel right and left,
Then as unto a ritual addressed,
The compass boxes to assure his rest;
This done, he sighs content and sleeps or seems —
He does most certainly — for now he dreams
And twitches, half complains as to insist,
We should have surely winged the pair I missed.
O God, I cannot think that I offend
If now I praise Thee, for so fine a friend!

And so in this my little kingdom rude,
As one renounced of strife, in solitude,
I am content upon this gorse to lie
And dream and drouse the vacant hour by;
But whiffs of perfume from the embers creep
Into my senses and I fall asleep
To wake, the sun three hours high, no more!
And we've to travel miles and miles before
We reach the road, for there's good ground in view,
That we must traipse, and leads we must persue!
Oh we must trudge, how far we'll hardly learn
For on the way we'll make full many a turn,

Criss cross the barrens, when the trails grow hot,
And comb some likely places for a shot.

We pause at length, foot weary, for "a blow",
To fit us for the final stretch, for lo,
The sun prepares again a golden crest,
For those blue ridges that we followed west;
And we must make the passage that pursues,
A crooked course that strangers oft confuse,
Though they by day those tangled woodlands cruise,
A path that we ourselves at night can lose;
So, as the lev'ling rays of ev'ning urge,
We haste our passage till we both emerge
On open ground, from whence we now descend,
With leisured footsteps to our journey's end!

The Ghost Ship

From dawn until late afternoon the sea
Has been as peaceful as the sea can be,
And little boats that seldom sail away
So far off shore as ours have sailed today
Intend, until the sun goes down, to stay
And fish the banks and ledges of the bay.
They cannot sense the sea's uneasy peace
Or how employment here so soon must cease,
For as wild things, alarmed of sound or sight
Beyond our eyes or ears take off in flight
The skiffs out there, we don't know why, take fright
And instant fly for shelter to the Bight;
Although the hagdown unrestrained of care,
Still skims and treads the water for his fare
And just as confident and just as sure,
The sharp-eyed gannet swoops again to score.

What harm hath chanced? What warning hath inclined
Those hardy little skiffs to change their mind?
Can it be she? But then how can it be
That we upon this cliff no ship may see?

"The Ghost Ship"

Ah yes, we see her now, and we may view
The ancient vessel and her ghastly crew
With eyes that see us not, but outward stare
As now she passes silent by us here;
A ship and company no one should mock,
For seas already rise about Shag Rock!
A topsail schooner makes toward the Bight;
She too has seen the vessel's ghostly light
And knows that far far greater ships than she
So warned, must flee tonight's Northeasterly.

The Salt Carriers

(To the memory of Victor Charles
Dawe killed in action 1914 - 1918)

Oh I remember long ago our sport,
When ships from foreign parts came to our port
And we would board them though they scarce had
   made
Their anchorage; unless we'd been delayed
By customs men suspicious of their trade,
Or as of course to get their port dues paid,
(Ah yes, 'twas later on we learned that some
Were partial to a glass of good ship's rum).
And with such diligence would poke and pry,
That none aboard could trick us by a lie;
And we would roam with hindrance none or let
Through ev'ry deck, each hold and lazarette
Moreover notwithstanding terror, oft
Would climb and creep and drag ourselves aloft
And "cap" the mainmast's or the mizzen's truck
Ashamed not to, or bound to show our pluck;
And there were big Norwegians, Danes and Swedes
Whose kindness would translate our English needs,

And others too with chanteys, songs and tales,
Like Griffiths men, who said they came from Wales.

Those ships had crossed the Western Ocean lade
In salt for fish, that would be split and made
By livyers in our coves and harbors, or
By planters up and down the Labrador;
And those same vessels would sail back again
All filled with fish for Italy and Spain,
Or bound for markets through Aegean seas
And friendly harbors of the Portugese.

'Twas for "the watches" that they struck their bells;
But there were famous friendly galley smells,
And they lived well; although we thought it strange
To see great big men tending on a range
And mixing duff or fixing soup or stew
And wondered how they knew just what to do;
But guessed their mothers gave them lessons home
'Gainst when they'd go to sea and on their own.

Square rigged they were, with lots of sail to darn,
And come those days with weather dry and calm,
The bosun'd hold the deck be-palmed to mend
Worn sails and torn that seemed to have no end;
And as I now recall those ancient times,
My heart to ev'ry sailing ship inclines;

For out of all the ships that put to sea,
The ship of sail finds her sufficiency
In what raw nature doth herself provide
In ev'ry latitude, of wind and tide;
(The skills of those who govern her and guide
Their fortitude and hardihood aside).
No engine hath this ship or like device,
Her sails with winds to fill them must suffice;
And if great gales from ev'ry quarter blow
To thwart her passage or to prove her foe,
She'll sail by all a thousand leagues to gain
One hundred only, constant in her aim;
And though beset by cont'ry tides and storm
Endangered oft, she'll yet achieve her bourne.

Oh ship of beauty, courage, faith, of sail,
Thou next-of-kin begotten of the gale!
Oh gallant vessel, if your sun must set
And commerce scratch your sailings or forget,
Will science all your gallantry efface,
Though tides swirl on in fog about Cape Race,
Or cosmic ventures bring your faith to scorn,
If winds torment the seas about Cape Horn?
No, not till all the seas refrain from storm
Or these themselves have altogether gone,
Nor till men's hearts, as of all feelings shorn,
To courage faith and valour cease to warm!

Observations on an Old Eating House

(To the memory of Richard Hibbs Esquire M.H.A.
Journalist, Humourist and Restaurateur)

This place is old, dependable, mature
And has wide preference.
Assured and confident,
It now seems almost anxious to reveal,
That which it once took measures to conceal,
Supporting charm.
The house has history
In honour, infamy.

'Twas held in high esteem by sailormen
Who gamed and won; but lost and lost again
And sometimes hocked small treasures to finance
And set them up, to take another chance.
'Twas said belongings theirs, can yet be seen
Stowed down below, that they'd looked to redeem:
Oh not for naught, 'twas called The Rogues Exchange
And bore repute for commerce black and strange!

Big Tom, 'tis thought, in this old place made good
So did the Lebanese in vending food,
And this and that and souvenirs;
But that was long ago,
And no one seems to know,
How many times the place changed hands until
The eating house, its furnishings, good will
And all advantages enjoyed therewith
Became the property of Jacob Smith
A Polish nobleman who sought no fame
In ancient titles or a jig-saw name.

He prospered mightily,
In his anonymity.
He brushed and cleansed the facade and within,
Removed or painted out the signs of sin,
And gave the tough and tainted place,
A quiet air and old world grace,
And carried on and after him his heirs,
The eating-house for half a hundred years;
And in that space, so far as it is known,
It has not changed in colour, pace or tone,
Or in much else, since Jacob first began,
To own and operate "The Merchantman".

The ancient street it faces is not wide,
Too narrow at the noontime for the tide

Of traffic, that is then upon it borne,
A street too old to alter, or reform.

Within is sanity.
The pace is here unhurried though not slow
Or slovenly. The patrons like it so,
And of vocations varied come and go.
They find the place agreeable and know,
That 'tis of those, a dwindling few who still
Take pains to gratify the mouths they fill,
By ancient art and culinary skill,
With due concern however for the till,
In right of management.
And patrons to this ancient house assign
An atmosphere compulsive but benign,
That I have not the language to define,
Somewhat like that we know on sav'ring wine,
Cooled for our lips, or feel as we resign,
To that tranquility of Sam's shoeshine.
Or yet that sense, with which you might compare,
The spell subversive of the barber's chair.

The city spreads and as it spreads inclines,
To build, rebuild on smooth efficient lines,
And "Restaurants", disposed to progress now,
The mass production of our age avow,
And choose your fare from pre-cooked goods in store,
Deprived of flavours or of taste obscure.

No patience these, with all their gilt and chrome,
With honest meals or kitchen-skills of home;
Though none the less, gratituities are still
In prime exchange for manners and good will!
But 'tis not so in ancient taverns where,
The pace remains unaltered year by year,
No change occurs in furniture and gear,
Unless by ordinary wear and tear,
Or by "improvements" which the City Hall,
Officially persuades them to instal;
Where blatant progress leaves no single sign,
Nor haste nor hurry dissipates the time.

But this old place hath beauty, we assess,
In vignettes vivid, free from strain and stress,
As lamps from age stained beams suspended shed
Their gentle light on tables damask spread,
And flames in forest incense constant trace,
Inconstant glories in the fireplace,
Where birch or wild witch-hazel flares and burns,
Or glows like tapers from perfumèd urns.

It hath no race or creed or colour ban,
It's open sesame, a gentleman!
So enter here, although it be confessed,
That you are scarce aware, whereof your quest,
Until you come upon it, as you find
Within these walls a tranquil state of mind!

94

And what shall be your profit, we agree
Proceeds from little that you here may see,
For little's here of merit we must own
In art or artistry approved or known,
Unless to this fair concept we assign:
Old prints and etchings rendered rare by time;
A famous ship in miniature, that made
Some sizzling voyages in the China trade.
A clock that ninety years by tick and chime
Has measured out with care the precious time,
That looks reflectively from yonder wall
On old and young and keeps account for all
Impartially, though some have cause for haste
Or think they have and others time to waste.

Of middle age, pre-emptive in conceit,
A tomcat dozes on the softest seat,
And only moves a greater ease to find,
Or stretch luxuriously paws fore and hind —
Lucullus named, the gentlest of his kind
By gen'rous girth and indolence refined.

But if you turn a while from all within,
You'll find an ancient with a violin,
Who sits without, and has, the weather fine,
For all of forty years in summertime.
And plays his robust airs, as one inclined,
To spend his largess solely for mankind;

Yet whence the fiddler comes, or where he goes,
His proper name, condition, no one knows.
Who cares? The question is impertinent;
The answer surely is inconsequent;
And in anonymity from day to day,
Responsive to a kindly sobriquet,
He tunes to Madrigal and Roundelay,
Exhausts his repetoire and goes his way.

The house is likeable;
And as within there may be those you'd see,
I bid you join with me its company.
For folk constituent of many sorts
From villages from towns and from the ports
Of half the world go in, as they incline
To tryst, confer, to bargain argue, dine,
Or enter it unconscious of design,
Or go as I to dream, sometimes to rhyme.

Of speed enamoured progress undefined,
By pressures goaded onward till the mind,
Must lose direction, we to day incline,
To proffer gracious living scanty time;
But here sustained by genial climes survive,
This one and that you thought not now alive.
Regard yon man there seated, too remote,
To trace his argument, but not to note,

How close the other listens, host or guest,
To ev'ry word he utters with respect,
And heeds his gestures too, as one who ought
Acknowledge ev'ry sign of profound thought;
How on the speaker's countenance he peers;
Aye, to his very silences gives ears!

Enough! while sage and sycophant share bread
And valiant wit must on applause be fed,
It can with little doubt or none be said,
Sam Johnson's not, nor is his Boswell dead.

By this man's gait his photographic gear,
His lofty looks and Himalayan air,
Outlandish rig, it doth indeed appear
That we have Marco Polo with us here.

Though it be trite and I but truth repeat,
Food's at its best, while we with others eat,
I cannot see, nor shall, how some divide
Attention fair 'twixt meals and news spread wide,
And I'm for him, who treats an honest meal
With courtesy; and eats it with zeal,
And as for news, though good or bad it be,
'Twill read I ween far better after tea.
Beyond that pair who bargain sell and note
The price agreed or prices that they quote,

You may observe a group that seems to me
Of their behaviour there, a family
Assembled for some purpose too obscure
Till he, no doubt the father, joins the four,
Comprising as, I think, you will agree,
A mother surely and her children three.
Two girls, a boy to manhood scarcely grown,
Who's likely on the hand of leaving home,
For see the fond attentions they employ
Embarrassing it seems the blushing boy,
Who frowns resentful of their overt care,
Their fuss and foolishness with him in here;
But love's compulsive and the time is short,
The siren screams. His vessel soon quits port
And soon he'll sail and soon his grief confess
For ev'ry frown frustrate of tenderness,
He lately gave.

Such places seem to ponder on the street,
Its pulse and beat and proffer it retreat,
From strife, in competence of drink and meat,
And traveller and passer-by entreat.

The town wherein we sojourn or reside,
The places that we frequent, may decide
Our way of life. Some buildings half enslave,
For by their grace and climate, we behave.

We sense a peace within and worship, while
Great seas lie calm and fertile valleys smile,
We know a wonder, awe and worship, where
Great mountains rise and climb to heights of fear.
We find conviction deepening beside
Great vaults and canyons fashioned by the tide,
Thus God is Nature! Man in creature part
Reflects the grace of his Creator's art
In divers ways, and we shall never know,
How much to art and artisans we owe,
In consolation, courage as we fare,
Through pain and loss, frustration and despair;
In sober conduct, in direction sane,
Through facile victories and mounting gain.

The brochures give their record scanty space
Or altogether fail their tale to trace;
But there are places that have won the way
To kind remembrance long beyond their day;
And though they shed no splendor on the town,
Or hold no right apparent to renown,
Not strange is it, if such, denied of fame,
The firm affection of the commons claim;
For these, hospitable and fair in gain,
The fond traditions of the town sustain,
And throughout years of peace and times of strife
Have hewn with constancy its way of life.

"When young and old abandon care"

May 24th (Trouter's Day in Newfoundland)

This is the twenty-fourth of May,
The Newfoundlander's holiday,
When young and old abandon care,
The pauper and the millionaire,
And to the ponds and rivers fare,
By limousine or by shank's mare.

And though you have but little time
To fish, and other days decline
To fish at all, come rain or shine
Today you're bound to wet your line.

And on tomorrow, round our way
I doubt not what a fellow'll say,
Or what conclusion he'll betray,
If asked what he did yesterday.
He'll think he hasn't heard aright,
And just say how he found 'em bite.

And though the winter lingering,
Still racks the ragged robe of Spring,
Tradition claims that we this way,
Observe the twenty-fourth of May.

The Rhyme of the Cutty Sark

I rhyme of ships that carry great square sails
That sog and stiffen, when it rains and hails;
Of men, who claw these in with broken nails
Against the threat'ning storms and rising gales.
I rhyme of seas, the breezes hardly fret,
Though ships proceed, their skuns'ls, skys'ls set,
I drift into the half forgotten past
Along the routes of lovely clipper craft,
Slim bowed and lissome, tall in yard and mast
And rhyme of her, the lovliest, and last.

(Old White Hat's Tale)

If you today cannot recall my name,
Obscured, as it may well be, by the fame
Of my great ship, I am indeed content,
As he, who is consoled by praises spent
Upon a child, who's honour is his own,
For I am old Jock Willis who was known

At Dunbarton, and 'long the River Clyde,
For sailing ships that travelled far and wide
Along the clipper routes; and I am he
Who owned the Cutty Sark, for 'twas for me
The ship was builded in accord with schemes
That I had patterned from my sailor dreams.
You see, I'd been myself sometime in sail,
And sensed the strategy of sea and gale,
And pondered often on designs to gain
A cargo ship so built as to attain
Advantage over seas; and to prevail
In winds, till these might to a capful fail,
And such proved she, I found 'twas even true,
That I had planned far better than I knew.
'Twas hard to think that I so soon would see
Coal eating steamers win our trade in tea
Along the routes to India, or how
Fast clippers could be ousted from Foochow,
And I was confident in 'sixty-nine
DeLesseps ditch would cave or clog with slime,
Was building too a ship of sail to reign
And beat the best on ev'ry clipper lane;
Though in the year the Cutty's keel was laid,
The Suez route had doomed our far East trade,
For sailing ships would still be bound to cope
With storms around Aghullas and Good Hope,
Whilst steamers, routed through the locks, could ply
In half our time from London to Shanghai.

Oh, she was staunch, was Cutty Sark, and sleek,
With jet black hull and decks of Burma teak:
In length, two hundred feet and twelve was she,
Of six and thirty beam; allegedly,
In all: nine hundred tons and sixty three,
About the same in gross capacity,
As her arch-rival the Thermopylae,
A clipper famed for speed on routes in tea.
And, I confess, I bore that ship in mind,
When, to my vessel, I the name assigned
Of "Cutty Sark," for then I haply thought
Of Robbie's nannie of the chemise short,
Who was so fleet and eager to prevail,
She overhauled Tam's mare and snatched her tail;
So with the witch pursuing, there aligned
Upon her stem-head, constant to remind
My vessel of her purpose to outsail
The ship Thermopylae and pluck the tail
Of that proud cock, the famous vessel wore,
As symbol of the championship she bore,
Or, of her undisputed right to reign
Above all sail on ev'ry clipper lane,
She floated out; but whilst upon the ways
She was a sight to charm a seaman's gaze:

In her fine hull were present those sure signs,
Distinctive of the clipper in her lines.

"She was a sight to charm a seaman's gaze"

I marvelled how her builders could endow
This vessel of such slenderness of bow,
With ample space, and yet capacity
To meet the stress and strain of wind and sea.
Rare grace swept in the lines of Cutty Sark,
Though she was staunch and sturdy as a bark:
Her lower planking, sheathed with copper, shone
Against her black topsides. She rested on,
As though a modelled glory to reveal,
A base constituent of rock elm keel.

The ship had many masters in her time:
George Moodie was her first, a friend of mine,
And who moreover, from the first to last,
Had watched and checked the building of the craft,
And he was sure the best went in the queen,
For we o'nights had long been used to scheme
On ways to build this ship of sail supreme,
Till she, as much as mine, became his dream;
And Moodie was in charge, when she left port
And tuned her up, and her shortcomings sought,
For by the sea alone, can we detect
The faults of square-rigged ships and these correct.
Such vessels are by seamen all confessed
Cantankerous, and mine was like the rest:
Her standing rigging wasn't set up taut,
Nor was her iron settled, as it ought;
But Moodie was a master such, that he,

For every fault, achieved a remedy;
Yet not in time to set a record by
Her voyage from London then, out to Shanghai.
Nor did she on returning, lade in tea,
Quite match the time set by Thermopylae;
But none the less the Cutty Sark somehow,
Upon her voyage to London from Foochow,
Then homeward bound and from her second run
To China, made the Spring of 'sev'nty-one,
Improved her ways, as minded to excel,
And raced the famous clipper Ariel
And, though she had not reached her sailing peak,
Made London, ere the other, by a week!
And Cutty Sark contended with, and got
The better of the great "Sir Lancelot."

Now up to then she had not met at sea
Her haughty rival, the Thermopylae;
Yet, as it chanced, the vessel that she sought
Turned up to lade at Shanghai, or the port
Where Cutty lay, and her she berthed beside;
And both left port upon the self same tide,
To London bound. That was in 'seventy-two
And ev'ry longshoreman and sailor knew,
These sailed a race, and coin of many lands,
Upon the finish, how and when, changed hands.

Of three days sailing little may we say,
For fog throughout obscured the vessels' way;
But when it cleared and all aboard could see,
Two miles, or nigh, ahead, Thermopylae,
The race began, and fought in weather fair,
For six and twenty days between the pair,
It left Thermopylae away to rear,
Four hundred miles; but in far better luck,
For she escaped the tempest, that then struck
At Cutty Sark, and frightful blasts that blew
Her canvas out, that they'd no time to clew
And smashed her gear, and boiling seas, that tore
Her rudder off; and 'way another bore,
That they had fashioned from spare spars in store,
And managed too, to lower and secure —
The great waves toppled constantly, to spew
In tons upon her deck, where strove her crew
With forge and iron stanchions to equip
Another yet, to guide their ailing ship;
But with a skill all seamen since have sung
A jury rudder there they built and hung
That bore the stress of ev'ry storm she fought
And ruled the Cutty's course to London Port.

Delayed by storm and slowed by damage, she
Could not o'ertake the fleet Thermopylae,
That had not met, nor had with tempest fought,
And would, one week, ere Cutty Sark, make port;

Though would this race in ev'ry phase unfold,
The Cutty Sark should most the honours hold;
Yet, notwithstanding all, "the rooster" stuck,
Affixed to proud Thermopylae's main truck!

Then Moodie left off sailing, for the cream,
He thought, of freights had surely gone to steam;
And though I didn't like their smoke and soot,
His views, I could not very well dispute,
For most our ships then on the old tea route,
Were glad to carry rice or wool or jute;
Or, their impov'rished owners to console,
Nigh anything that offered, down to coal.
And sailing masters, too, were hard to find,
I mean the good, for late, nigh all inclined
To look ahead toward a better wage,
And with the lines of steamships to engage.

Her Master next was Captain Moore, a man,
Who saw that Cutty Sark was spic and span,
Before he took her out. Of great repute was he,
And under him, she met great clippers three:
Titania, (and with her loading tea
At Shanghai) Lancelot, Thermopylae,
From whence they left, in seeming rivalry,
And sailed together down the China Sea;
But Cutty Sark, as though disposed to doom,
Encountered, once again, the wild typhoon,

And though she beat the others sailing home,
Thermopylae retained the Clipper Throne.
With Masters good and bad and lacking drive,
From 'seventy-three, right up to 'eighty-five,
The Cutty Sark but rarely seemed to thrive
And managed, only barely, to survive;
Though under Wallace, (aye a fine man too),
When cargoes offering in tea were few,
She made fair freights in the Australian trade,
In wool; and under him moreover made
The western ocean, at a clip to praise:
New York to London, in just nineteen days!
But Cutty Sark, the lovely ship, we knew,
Without affection from her master, crew,
Unloved by those whose duty was to show
Attention to, and on her to bestow
A little paint and polish here and there,
Became a tramp, of prospect drab and drear,
And not unlike a woman, once thought fair,
But unattractive grown in lack of care
Or kindliness, for we might well confess
That beauty thrives on love and tenderness.

And if, my masters, I may yet digress,
We do not know and we may never guess,
How oft we of indifference suppress,
Some spark divine or nascent loveliness.

"And sail her into everlasting fame"

Yet Cutty Sark in case most desperate,
Would yet retrieve her honour and estate,
For in the year of 'eighty-five, there came
A man aboard the vessel by the name
Of Richard Woodget, to confirm her claim
And sail her into everlasting fame.
No reckless driver, though discerning bold,
He would give everything her spars could hold.
If strong of will, he was of manner bright
And humorous, and for his own delight
And theirs, the tedium of their voyages long,
Would join his crew, to while away, in song,
And on occasions fit, and for sound cheer,
In other pleasantries of theirs would share;
And he, as well, still looking to their good,
Concerned himself with bettering their food;
Yet never pampered nor let them construe,
That they had gotten more than, he thought due,
And tasks would set them, that they might atone
For past neglects, that none would dare postpone:

Bedraggled rigging he would not condone,
Or dirty decks, that they should holystone,
And all he asked of them, and more, was done,
For by his discipline the brasses shone,
The sails repaired, her stays and shrouds renewed,
Until she seemed a ship, by others crewed.

Her boys behaved like old deep water men
And old hasbeens became as men again,
Of steel. No longer slovenly and soft,
In spirits high, they hopped, when sent aloft,
And with this man as master, ev'ry trip
The Cutty Sark became a better ship.
The tattered tramp regained respect and shone,
As splendid nigh, as when at Dunbarton,
She slid upon her ways and out to sea
To vanquish, as I thought, Thermopylae.
And as the vessel voyaged from sloth redeemed
And squalor cleansed, she prospered till it seemed
My trust had been sustained; or that my dream
Had substance gained; and she was Clipper Queen;
Had not the Cutty only lately made
Some sizzling trips in our Australian trade;
For though we had reduced the vessel's sails,
To cut expense, she sped from New South Wales
To England, in but twelve and three score days;
And on to Sydney, as the record says,
In fifty eight, all done without such aids
As stuns'ls, held in favour with light trades.

Her crew, that stood at nine and twenty, when
She first had sailed, was then but nineteen men,
For nigh all Shanghai charters, as we've seen
Had gone from sailing vessels, on to steam.

And she had suffered with the rest, and hence
Her sails had been reduced to save expense.
But Cutty Sark had come back to regain
Her prestige and her place upon the main;
Albeit, she must surely meet again
The ship Thermopylae, for if the twain
Have twice contended, 'tis abundant plain,
That neither o'er the other can maintain
Conclusive victory, despite the lead,
The Cutty Sark had held and yet might plead,
Of full four hundred miles, ere hurricane
Had struck at her and stripped her of her gain,
Disabling her: but 'tis by no means meet
To argue victory, or excuse defeat,
For ships, if they must use the winds and seas,
Must bear the whims and caprices of these,
And though the cyclone strike at one, to thwart,
And let the other voyage, unscathed, to port;
No ship that sails hath yet safe conduct borne,
Or holds of right, the deference of storm.
And 'till they meet, the issue to decide,
Betwixt the twain, opinion must divide
In ev'ry foc'sle, the oceans wide,
And ev'ry sailors' boarding house beside,
And if for one, ten thousand may contend,
As many tongues, the other will defend.

'Twas in Australia and at Jackson Port
They met, as though they had each other sought,
And sailed together on the self same morn
Along smooth seas, by mod'rate breezes borne.
Australian shores have scarce commenced to fail,
When one, and soon the other, spreads more sail
To take advantage of the steady gale.
Thermopylae however to prevail,
Against her adversary lifts skysail,
Of winds no doubt the better to avail;
And yet a further vantage to attain,
She bends her stuns'ls, but 'tis all in vain.
The slim bowed Cutty, as an arrow speeds,
And at the dawning comfortably leads;
Although my ship aware of her arrears
And costs to cut, no fancy canvas bears.
But in late afternoon, the second day,
The wind so veers or alters in such way,
'Tis found the tales long heard are well nigh true
Of what the great Thermopylae can do,
Upon a windward thrash; and how she's won
And earned her fame by many a record run;
For in this wind, the third morn of the race
Thermopylae has taken up first place;
But loses out upon the fourth, for then
The Cutty finds her fav'ring wind again
And from her adversary draws away
To meet her, when or how, none yet may say,

"The slim bowed Cutty, as an arrow speeds"

For there is many and many a league to go,
Rough seas to buck and sails to reef and stow,
Upon a voyage where vessels must abide
The vagaries of weather, wind and tide
And terrors, that the oceans may devise,
And hurl upon them, should their wrath arise;
And there's no telling when they'll find relief
From hardtack, water and from cold salt beef,
Or when her hands will find dry bunks below,
For he'll be "cracking on" blow high or low.

As athletes by their wiles and motions fleet
Fierce adversaries ponderous defeat,
She circumvents great waves that threaten ill
Or outmanoeuvres of her very will.
Like some tall knight who doth the field engage
She runs the gauntlet of an ocean's rage.
Yet on she sails, and on, and on, and on,
Till as in effort spent, her spirit gone,
Or stricken sudden of some grievous harm,
She stumbles limp upon sea, flat calm!

She's struck the doldrums and her anxious crew,
With scant resource or little left to do,
Of ancient custom, whistle for a wind,
And unsuccessful, in this way, to find
The means to rouse her or afford release,
They urge her by a dolorous "ash breeze"

Till, lo a languid air; but ere the shout
That hails it, dies, this Sou'west flaw blows out.
And all day long and night becalmed she lies;
But on the morrow, nearing noon she slides
Before a breath that rallies to a breeze,
And Cutty Sark picks up her heels and flees!

Too long the tale and tedious for you
Of storms and trials that she battles through
And of the distances from day to day
She sails to take the clipper crown away,
For Woodget has, as he has promised, struck
"That bauble" from Thermopylae's main truck.
And if you think she wins by fluke or freak,
Or I, of fondness or of bias speak,
Then go, my masters, to your books and seek,
For you will learn, she wins by full a week!
And you should know that of her right to reign,
As queen of clippers, when she leaves again
The port of London, for the Far East seas,
She flies at her main truck, a gold chemise!
For I, John Willis, known as "Old White Hat",
This day awaiting, look myself to that!

(End of Old White Hat's Tale)

This was the greatest race of all between
The clipper ships, indeed the last, for steam

Had taken over ev'ry clipper lane
And left few freights to sail of any gain;
Though Cutty Sark, in wool, remained in trade,
And noted voyages to Australia made;
Why under Woodget, on a Sydney run,
She raced a steamer into port and won;
Yet barely did she manage to survive
The one-way battle until 'ninety-five,
When pushed and pressed of harsh economies,
She passed into the hands of Portuguese.

And one by one deprived by steam of gains,
The clippers quit their ancient trading lanes:
Some were dismasted and allowed to rot,
Some wrecked, or scrapped, in worthlessness forgot,
And others sold for use as barges, or
For office else, as lowly and as poor.
The "Ariel" went down somewhere alone,
"Sir Lancelot" was stricken by cyclone,
And foundered off Sand Heads, to taunt her past,
A load of salt to sink her at the last.

As for Thermopylae, when sold, she went
In service of a foreign Government,
And as the Pedro Nunes at the time,
Was scuttled at the age of thirty-nine;
But Cutty Sark, as fashioned to defy
Misfortune and disaster, would not die

And though through years grown shabby of neglect,
She yet was handsome and compelled respect;
And when she hove into a British port,
In course of business, or, there haven sought,
Old clipper hands and sailormen were fain
To yarn in fond remembrance of her fame;
Though prone to raise in argument again,
What all of them were anxious to maintain.

And on she sailed until the year 'sixteen,
When Cutty Sark in other guise was seen,
For she was then rerigged a barquentine,
To bear division of resources lean;
You see, the ship had lost her masts in storm
And spars were scanty, in the lands wartorn;
Yet none, save lubbers, failed to recognize
The clipper lines, despite her altered guise.

Nor did the longer foreign sounding name
She wore in 'twenty-two, conceal her fame
From Captain Wilfred Dowman, or deny
The glory of her lines to his shrewd eye,
For he proposed to buy and to equip
The storied clipper as a training ship,
And in due course, as this old seaman planned,
The Cutty Sark regained her native land,
And to this day, she lives in Britain, where
They've built a home for her at Greenwich Pier,

"To yarn in fond remembrance of her fame"

And you may see the great old vessel there,
Exemplar of the fastest and most fair,
Of sailing ships. She's ninety now, or more,
All active years, save those few years ashore
On dry dock here, for not till 'fifty-three
Did Cutty Sark retire from the sea.
Unscathed, she came through nights of flame and fear;
Although she berthed or lay at moorings near,
Where many a ship was broken or went down,
Beneath the blitz on Thames by London Town;
And now as one, who's earned a nation's care
For service rendered, or achievements rare,
She rests in age, though sound as she is fair,
A grace remaining from a vanished year.

IN RETIREMENT

And many come, and view a while and go
And pay fair tribute to a nation's show.
A few, if unobtrusive, in the train
With more than passing interest remain.
These be, it seems, the thoughtful leisured, or
Old sailors now retired to the shore,
Who wait until the witching twilight falls
To hear, I think, again her windlass pawls
Some wistful chanty and the tramp of feet,
As seamen turn about their capstan beat

Until the anchor's raised, the one they've hurled
And chantied up from ports of half the world;
To view aloft the vessel's slender spars
Up to their trucks amid the gath'ring stars.

And if amongst this little group there be
Old hands of hers who served in wool or tea,
No more of course than youngsters at the time
She sizzled from the Lizzard to the Line
Or made her easting south of forty-five,
Though old men now, if they be yet alive.
They'll ponder here till river mists restore
T'gansl's, royals (mizzen, main and fore)
Till on she sails with all her plain sails trimmed
And as of old again outsails her wind.,

But though they now may wander where they please
And choose the temperate and fav'ring breeze,
They'll sail her on and wheresoe'er 'twill seem
The cargo's destined, though they only dream,
And, as by manifest, assuredly
Take to the old time routes of wool or tea.
Long disciplined to hardship, they'll evade
The fav'ring vigor of the constant trade,
And as bereft of choice or sailing room,
Engage in battle with the wild typhoon,
And in the shock and passage of the bout,
Blow her brave topsails from their bolt ropes out.

124

They too will voyage again in wastes forlorn
And hear the shiv'ring lookout's doleful horn
Inquiring constant whilst they skun their way
Through fog-bound seas and bergs that drift and stray
A'port and starboard, as in warning calls
The penguin, flound'ring on his polar walls.

And they will climb aloft in storm again
And mount the swaying yards to tug and strain
On sodden stubborn canvas that they stow,
As lifts and rolls the deck awash below.
They take what comes to drown them or to freeze,
And storm the kingdom of the westerlies,
And as assigned to man the flooded waist,
Strain on her lee or on her weather brace
With knifing squalls or hailstones to outface,
And hardblown spume, whereof they waking taste!

But they return, as birds to favoured trees,
To ponder here, recalling at their ease
The Roaring Forties or the Tropic seas
In anger rampant or restrained at peace;
Withal to measure and to contemplate
And share with pride in her achievements great.

L'ENVOI

I rhyme for ships, for ships are ever fair,
And they have been accustomed long to bear

For man his commerce and with him to share
In perils diverse and deserve his care;
Moreover, to the mightiest, they feel
Man's lightest mood, obedient to the wheel,
And seem inclined with all aboard to strive
As though aware nor ship nor crew survive
Disaster else, and as I've rhymed for you
O Cutty Sark, I've thought of ships I knew,
That were by storm or misadventure cast
On reefs or shoals and there held hard and fast,
Beyond the strength or competence of tides
To lift their keels, or right their listless sides;
And I recall these best, I think, at night,
As I remember them beneath moonlight
Along our Southern Shore, or just at day,
When in the fog of easterlies they lay,
And I have heard the seas still violate
Their crooked stanchions, struts and rusting plate.

And even now, as on these ships I muse,
I'm wond'ring what became of all their crews,
Did these of hardship, borne in peril, choose
To quit the sea, as chastened men quit booze?
Not all, I ween. Disasters may divide
The vet'rans from the greenhorns and untried;
But masters, mates and bosuns and old hands,
Who are no more than sojourners on lands

And needs must find some roof upon the seas
Or other habitations, like to these,
They've lost, sign on, and on, and on, again,
'Till ships have no more use for honest men;
And they moreover injuries defy,
Until they sicken of their years and die,
Or from their meagre wages hoard enough,
To deal in souvenirs, tobacco, snuff
Beside the waterfront; content to be
Consoled and nurtured by their mother sea.

So here's to you, and such as have grown old
And find, O Cutty Sark, the pot of gold
At rainbow's end, in plain tranquility,
Somewhere along the fringes of the sea.

Paul Parsons 62